SCIENCE
IS EVERYWHERE

FORCES IN ACTION

Balance, motion and levers

Rob Colson

WAYLAND

First published in Great Britain
in 2017 by Wayland
Copyright © Hodder and Stoughton, 2017

Wayland
An imprint of Hachette
Children's Group
Part of Hodder and Stoughton
Carmelite House
50 Victoria Embankment
London EC4Y 0DZ

Executive editor: Adrian Cole
Produced by Tall Tree Ltd
Written by: Rob Colson
Designer: Ben Ruocco

ISBN: 978 1 5263 0498 8
10 9 8 7 6 5 4 3 2 1

An Hachette UK Company
www.hachette.co.uk
www.hachettechildrens.co.uk

Printed and bound in China

The website addresses (URLs) included
in this book were valid at the time of
going to press. However, it is possible
that contents or addresses may have
changed since the publication of this book.
No responsibility for any such changes
can be accepted by either the author or
the Publisher.

MIX
Paper from
responsible sources
FSC® C104740
FSC
www.fsc.org

t-top, b-bottom, l-left, r-right, c-centre,
front cover-fc, back cover-bc
All images courtesy of Dreamstime.com,
unless indicated:
Inside front Artem Egorov; fc, bc
Pablo631; fctl, 21tr Kikovicimg; fctr
Ssuaphoto; fcbr Jabiru; bctl Sergiy1975;
bctr Jeffwilliams87; bccl, 28b Dr. Ing.
h.c.F. Porsche AG; 1bl, 21l Clivia; 4l
Ilona75; 5tl, 19cr Paulmichaelhughes;
5t, 19c Andreadonetti; 5cl Cglightning;
5cr Prillfoto; 5br Paprikaa; 6cl, b, 7tl
Mrincredible; 6bc, 7c Elena Torre; 7bc
Merfin; 7bl Gstudioimagen; 8tl CC BY
4.0 http://creativecommons.org/licenses/
by/4.0/; 8bl Photka; 8bcl Vectorlibellule;
9t NASA; 9bl Dedmazay; 10b Stoyan
Haytov; 11c McLaren Automotive
Ltd; 12-13c Aprescindere; 12-13b, 28c
Evgenii Naumov; 14c Bruder; 16t
Parkinsonsniper; 16b Mandj98; 17t
Design56; 18b Georgsv; 19bl Robot100;
19bl Mitch1921; 20t Alancotton; 20tl
zenwae; 20b Clarita; 22-23, 30b Alexmax;
23bl, 31tr Blueringmedia; 24cl, b Berc;
25tr shutterstock/Nicholas Piccillo; 25bl
Dennis Crow; 26-27b shutterstock/
blambca; 27tr Funwayillustration; 28tr
shutterstock/Dundanim; 28tc Forplayday;
29tr Nikmerkulov; 30tc Travismanley;
30tr Photka; 30tr Pincarel; 32t
Stylephotographs

Contents

Feel the force

Forces are pushes and pulls, which change an object's shape, speed or direction of movement.

"We've got you now!"

Force **X 2**   Force **X 2**

Tug of war

If the force with which each tug of war team pulls is equal,

they will not move.

But as soon as one team starts pulling harder than the other, they will all move in the direction that team is pulling.

"Hey, that's not fair!"

Force **X 2**   Force **X 3**

Newton's laws

In the 17th century, the English scientist Sir Isaac Newton (1642–1727) produced three laws of motion, which describe how forces work.

1 An object at rest will stay at rest, and a moving object will keep moving in a straight line, unless a force acts on it. This means that, if a car travelling at 50 km/h comes to a sudden halt by hitting a wall, the passengers inside will continue moving at 50 km/h without a seatbelt or airbag to stop them.

2 The force (F) acting on an object is equal to its mass (m) times its acceleration (a):

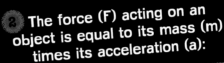

$$F = ma$$

This means that the heavier an object, the more force is needed to move it.

3 If one body exerts a force on another object (action), the second object will exert an equal force in the opposite direction (reaction). This is the key to how a rocket works: it pushes out gas at high speed, and this is matched by an equal force pushing the rocket forwards.

Force on rocket (reaction)

Force on gas (action)

TRY THIS

To see Newton's third law in action, blow up a balloon then let it go. The force of the air rushing out of the balloon will produce a reaction that sends it flying across the room.

Weighed down

A force of attraction exists between all objects. Called gravity, the strength of this force depends on the objects' mass and their distance from one another. The more massive the objects and the closer they are, the stronger the gravity. Earth is so massive that its gravitational pull is strong enough to keep us on the ground.

Mass or weight?

Mass is a measure of the amount of matter an object contains, and is measured in units called kilograms (kg). When we weigh ourselves, we are measuring the force of our mass pushing on the scales as gravity pulls us down. This force is measured in Newtons (N). One Newton is equal to the force required to accelerate an object with a mass of 1 kg by **1 metre per second per second ($1 m/s^2$).**

On Mercury,
a person with a mass of
100 kg
will exert a force of
380 N

An object's weight depends on the strength of gravity. The more massive the planet, the stronger its gravity.

On Earth,
a person with a mass of
100 kg
will exert a force of
980 N

On Jupiter,
a person with a mass of
100 kg
will exert a force of
2,300 N

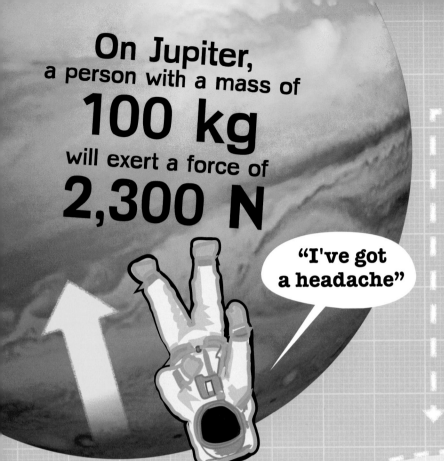

"I've got a headache"

Equal speeds

A ball with a mass of **2 kg** will be pulled by gravity with twice the force of a ball with a mass of **1 kg**. However, the **2 kg** ball also needs twice the force to achieve the same acceleration as the **1 kg** ball. This means that gravity on Earth makes all objects accelerate at the same rate (called '**g**'), which is measured at

$$9.8 \text{ m/s}^2.$$

Italian scientist Galileo Galilei (1564–1642) showed this by dropping two spheres of

different mass at the same time

from the top of the Leaning Tower of Pisa. As Galileo had predicted, both spheres hit the ground at the same time.

"I told you so!"

Some objects, such as feathers, fall much more slowly due to air resistance, but with no air, a feather and a hammer would fall at the same speed. In 1971, astronaut David Scott proved this in an experiment on the Moon. He dropped a feather and a hammer, and with no air to slow the feather down, both fell with exactly

the same acceleration.

A universal force

Sir Isaac Newton was the first person to work out that gravity is a universal force. The same force that makes an apple fall to the ground also keeps the Moon in orbit around Earth and the planets in orbit around the Sun.

Constant pull

As the Moon moves, Earth's gravity pulls it towards Earth. This changes its direction so that it moves around Earth in an orbit.

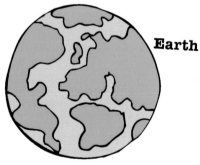

Orbit of the Moon around Earth

Pull of the Moon and Earth on each other

Earth

Moon

Pull of gravity changes the path of the Moon

Without Earth's gravity, Newton's first law states that the Moon would fly off in a straight line.

Path the Moon would take without Earth

Black hole

Location of our Solar System

Our galaxy, the Milky Way, rotates around a massive central black hole. Without its gravity, the stars would all fly away from one another.

TRY THIS

This is an experiment to do in the park! Tie a tennis ball to a piece of string a couple of metres long. Hold the other end of the string and swing the ball above your head so that it makes a big horizontal circle around you. Feel the effort it takes to hold on as it gets faster. The faster it swings the more force is needed to change its direction. If let go, it will fly off in a straight line.

Friction

A force pushing an object will accelerate the object for ever, unless another force opposes it. All movement on Earth is opposed by a force called friction. Friction is caused when a moving surface rubs against another surface.

Interstellar

In space, there is almost no friction, and a relatively small force can accelerate an object forever. If we ever send people to distant stars, the best acceleration for the spacecraft will be a **constant 1 g (9.8 m/s^2) – equivalent to the force of gravity on Earth.** With this acceleration, the space travellers would feel the same weight as they feel on Earth. For the first half of the journey the **spacecraft accelerates at 1 g**, and for the second half, its thrusts turn around and it **decelerates at 1 g** to reach a stop at its destination. With this method, a spacecraft could reach the star system Sirius, **8.6 light-years away,** in just ten years. That's a distance more than

200 million times farther than the Moon!

Sliding friction

Two surfaces in contact with one another produce **sliding friction**. Here, a large area is in contact, producing lots of friction.

Force ▶▶   Motion ▶▶

◀◀◀ Sliding friction

Rolling friction

Friction can be reduced by **rolling an object** rather than sliding it. When an object rolls, only a small area is in contact.

Force ▶▶   Motion ▶▶

◀◀◀ Rolling friction

Earth

1 g acceleration

5 years

Aerodynamic

Friction caused by **moving through the air** is known as air resistance. Sports cars such as the McLaren P1 are designed in a wedge shape so that they cut a path through the air with the minimum air resistance. This is called an **aerodynamic shape.**

The car sits low to the ground, and air is directed smoothly over the top.

To see how rolling reduces friction, slide a book across a table. Note how quickly it stops. Now lay a couple of round pencils parallel to one another under the book and try again. The same force should send the book flying off the end of the table.

"Usain Bolt, eat your heart out!"

1 g deceleration

5 years

Sirius

Putting on the brakes

A moving object has a form of energy called kinetic energy. Brakes slow the object down using friction to remove this kinetic energy.

Stopping distance

The distance it takes a car to brake to a stop contains two parts:

Thinking distance

The first part is the **thinking distance**. This is due to the time between the driver seeing the danger and applying the brakes. During this time, the car keeps going at the same speed. The thinking time for an average driver is about **$2/3$ second.**

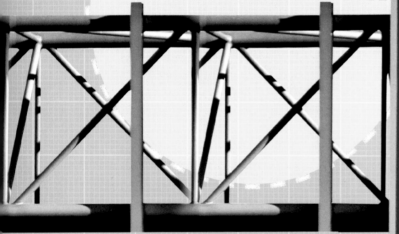

Thinking distance   Braking distance

20 km/h: 4 m + 2 m = 6 m
(One and a half car lengths)

**40 km/h:
8 m + 8 m = 16 m**
(Four car lengths)

Kill the speed

If a person is hit by a car travelling at **30 km/h**, this is the equivalent force to hitting the ground after a fall from a first floor window. At **40 km/h**, it is equivalent to falling from a third floor window at twice the height, which is far more dangerous. For this reason, speed limits in urban areas are a lot lower.

TRY THIS

Parachutes are brakes that slow down objects by increasing their air resistance.

What you need:
Some plastic bags of different sizes, scissors, string, a weight (such as an action figure)
1. Cut out a large square from the plastic bag and trim the edges to make an octagon (an eight-sided shape).
2. Cut a small hole near the edge of each side.
3. Attach eight pieces of string of the same length to each hole. Tie them all to the weight.

Try parachutes of different sizes. The larger the surface area of the parachute, the more it will slow your object down.

Braking distance

The second part is the distance it takes for the brakes to stop the car. Kinetic energy increases by a square of speed. This means that a car moving at **40 km/h** has **four times the kinetic energy** of a car moving at **20 km/h**, and its breaking distance will be four times further. In good conditions, brakes decelerate the car at a rate of about **7 m/s²**, meaning that the car's speed reduces by **7 m/s per second.**

Wet roads

On wet roads, braking distances are much longer. This is because the water reduces the friction between the car's tyres and the road.

80 km/h: 16 m + 36 m = 52 m
(Thirteen car lengths)

Lift-off

Birds and aeroplanes stay in the air because of a force called lift. A wing produces lift as the object moves forwards in two ways: its aerofoil shape and its angle of attack.

Aerofoil

An aerofoil has a curved upper surface and a flat lower surface, which causes air flowing over the wing to travel faster than air under the wing. The faster-moving air is at a lower pressure, meaning that the air below pushes the wing up.

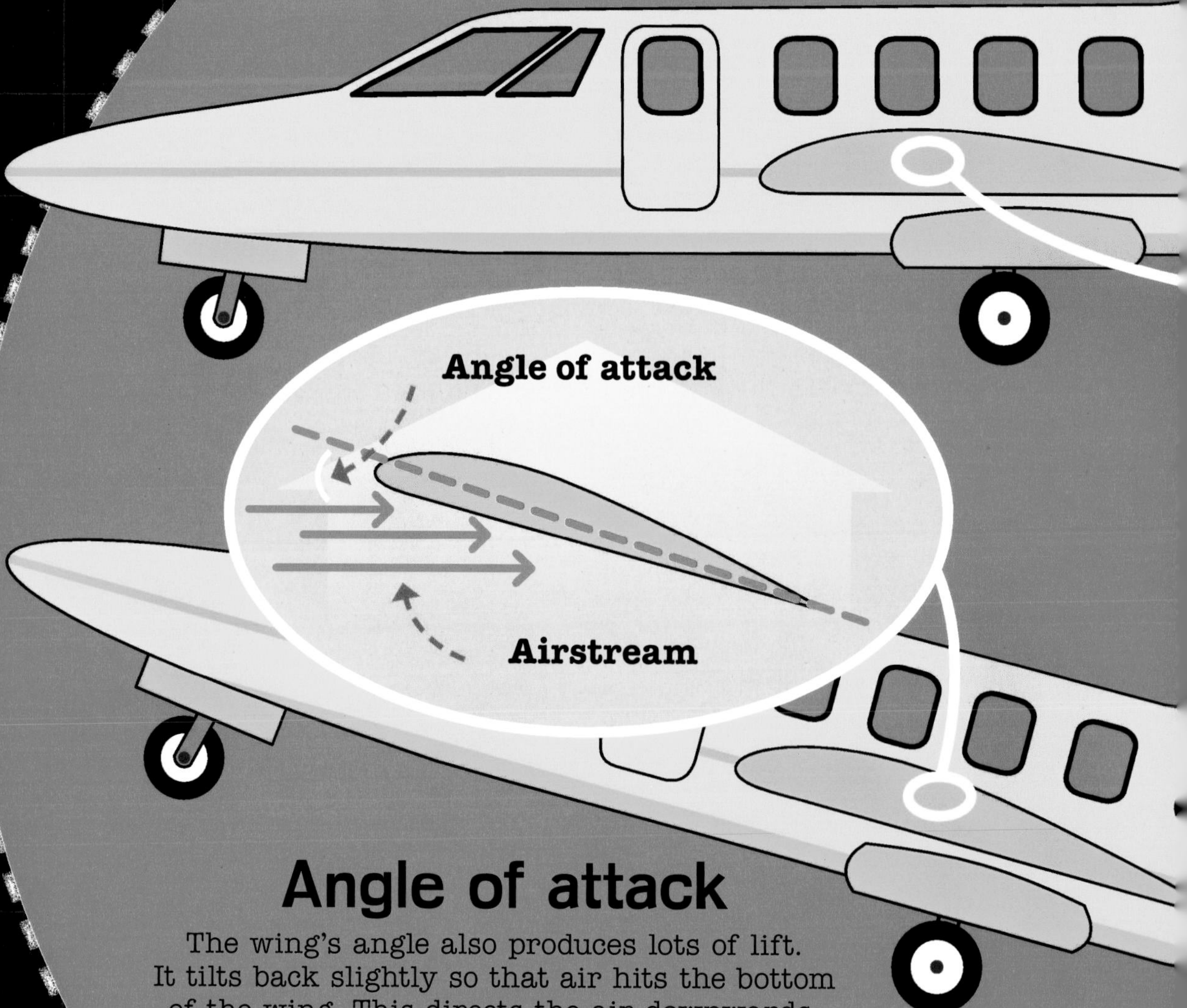

Angle of attack

Airstream

Angle of attack

The wing's angle also produces lots of lift. It tilts back slightly so that air hits the bottom of the wing. This directs the air downwards, and using Newton's third law, produces an equal and opposite force pushing the wing up.

Take two pieces of paper, one in each hand. Hold them a few centimetres apart under your mouth. Do you think they will come apart or move closer if you blow between them? By blowing between the sheets, you are making the air move faster, which lowers its pressure. The higher pressure of the still air on either side pushes the sheets of paper together.

Lower pressure

Higher pressure

Bird power

Birds use both aerofoil-shaped wings and angle of attack to produce lift. They also produce extra lift by flapping their wings. The shape of a bird's wings varies depending on what kind of flying it needs to do.

Albatross

Long, narrow wings are good for **slowly gliding**

Short, pointed wings are good for **high speeds**

Peregrine falcon

Crow

Short, rounded wings are good for **changing direction** in tight spaces

1

Levers

Levers are simple machines that help us to move things. The object to be moved is called the load. The force used to move the object is called the effort. The load and effort are combined with a fulcrum to produce movement.

Class 1 lever

The fulcrum is placed between the load and the effort. The movement of the load is in the opposite direction to the effort. The longer the effort arm is compared to the load arm, the less effort is required to move the load.

L   F   E

Load   Effort

Fulcrum

Scissors
The load is nearer to the fulcrum than the effort, which increases the force on the load.

Class 2 lever

Here, the load is placed between the effort and the fulcrum. The load moves in the same direction as the effort, but over a smaller distance. Class 2 levers are good for lifting heavy loads.

Effort   Load

Fulcrum

Wheelbarrow
The load is lifted a small distance by a long movement of the effort.

L

F

Class 3 lever

The effort is between the load and the fulcrum. Load and effort move in the same direction, and the load moves over a longer distance than the effort, with less force. Class 3 levers are good for picking up something small or delicate.

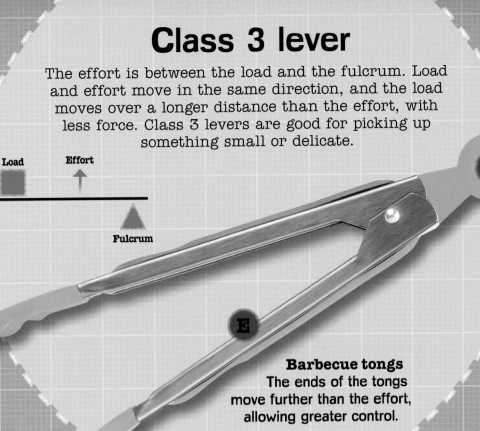

Load   Effort

Fulcrum

E

L

Barbecue tongs
The ends of the tongs move further than the effort, allowing greater control.

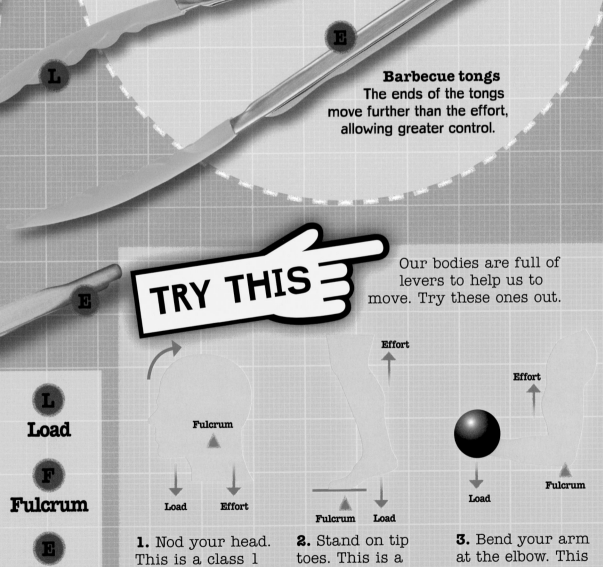

E

TRY THIS

Our bodies are full of levers to help us to move. Try these ones out.

L
Load

F
Fulcrum

E
Effort

Fulcrum

Load   Effort

1. Nod your head. This is a class 1 lever.

Effort

Fulcrum   Load

2. Stand on tip toes. This is a class 2 lever.

Effort

Load

Fulcrum

3. Bend your arm at the elbow. This is a class 3 lever.

17

Rolling along

A wheel moving around a central axle is a simple machine that turns sliding friction into rolling friction.

Wheel

Rolling, rolling, rolling

The mosaic above dates from **4,500 years ago.** It shows a Sumerian war chariot. Its wheels are solid, and the chariot would have been relatively slow.

Axle

Spokes

About 500 years later, the **spoked wheel** was invented in Central Asia. Wooden spoked wheels were lightweight but strong. A metal rim was later added to make the wheels **more durable.**

Pulleys

Pulleys are sets of wheels and axles that change the direction of a force and help to lift heavy weights. In a pulley system, **the more wheels you use, the less force is needed** to lift the same weight, but the force needs to travel a longer distance.

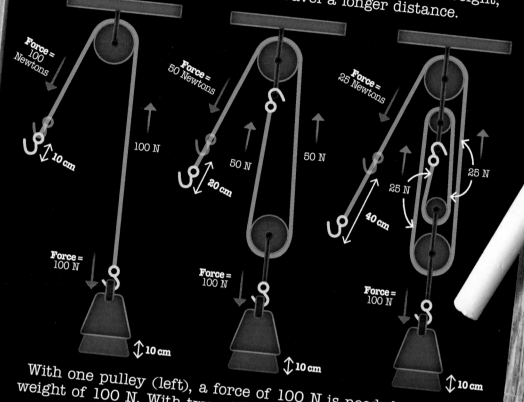

Force = 100 Newtons

100 N

10 cm

Force = 100 N

10 cm

Force = 50 Newtons

50 N   50 N

20 cm

Force = 100 N

10 cm

Force = 25 Newtons

25 N   25 N

40 cm

Force = 100 N

10 cm

With one pulley (left), a force of 100 N is needed to lift a weight of 100 N. With two pulleys (middle), 50 N is needed. With four pulleys (right) 25 N is needed.

TRY THIS

Just one pulley on its own can make lifting much easier, as we find it easier to pull down than to pull up.

What you need:
A rope, a heavy book, a railing or bannister.
1. Tie the book to the rope. See how it feels to lift the book using the rope.
2. Now throw the rope over the railing and try pulling down on it. Is it easier to lift?

Sloping surfaces

A ramp is a smooth surface that is tilted at an angle. It is also known as an inclined plane.

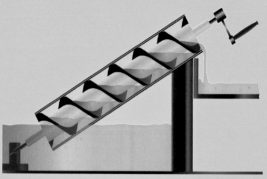

Screws

A screw is an inclined plane wrapped around a cylinder. It turns 'rotating' movement into 'straight' movement.

An Archimedes screw lifts water from one level to another.

A helter-skelter is a screw that allows people to slide safely in circles, rather than fall straight down.

Distance lifted

Weight

Direction of movement

Distance travelled

Gradient

Ramps allow us to lift heavy loads using less effort by applying the effort over a longer distance. The angle of the ramp is called its gradient. The lower the gradient, the longer the distance and the smaller the effort required.

Roads wind up steep mountains to reduce the gradient, allowing cars to drive up the hill, and also to descend safely.

Wedges

A wedge is an inclined plane that moves through something else. An axe is an example of a wedge.

"It's high up here!"

The axe changes the direction of the force to push out on the wood and slice through it.

TRY THIS

A doorstop is a kind of wedge. Take a doorstop and push it under a door. The further in you push it, the greater the force pushing up at the door and down at the ground. How far did you need to push it in to stop the door from moving?

Get in gear

Gears are toothed wheels that move power from one part of a machine to another and change the speed of rotation.

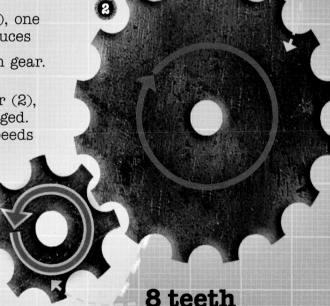

❶ 16 teeth

16 teeth

The simplest gear system contains two gears: a **driver** gear and a **driven** gear. The teeth on each gear are spaced at the same distance so that they interlock.

If the gears are the same size (1), one rotation of the driver gear produces **one rotation** of the driven gear.

If one gear is larger than the other (2), the speed of rotation can be changed. The difference between the two speeds is called the **gear ratio**. You can work out the gear ratio by counting the number of teeth. This gear system has a gear ratio of 2. One rotation of the large gear produces **two rotations** of the small gear.

❷

8 teeth

With a two-gear system, the direction of rotation of the driver gear is **reversed** for the driven gear. To change the direction back again, a third gear needs to be added between them.

24 teeth

Rack and pinion

In a rack and pinion gear system, a circular 'pinion' is connected to a straight 'rack'. Rack and pinion systems are used on railways where the trains go up steep hills. They stop the train from sliding backwards.

Pinion

Rack

TRY THIS

Changing gears on a bicycle changes the ratio between the driver gear attached to the pedals and the driven gear on the rear wheel. This is a two-gear system with the addition of a chain. Take a bicycle with derailleur gears and turn it upside-down. Count the number of teeth on the driver gears and the driven gears. **What are the possible ratios? Which gear would you use to ride up steep hills?**

23

Forces
in sport

Ready, set, go!

At the start of a race, a sprinter needs to get up and running as quickly as possible. The **starting blocks are adjustable**. The sprinter angles the blocks in the direction she want to move, so that the reaction to the pressure on the blocks gives

maximum force
in the correct direction.

From the set position...

...the sprinter pushes forwards at an angle of 45 degrees

45°

24

How to pitch a fastball

In baseball, a fastball is a pitch that is thrown as fast as possible, sometimes more than 150 kph. To produce this speed, the pitcher needs to use his whole body.

1. The wind up
The pitcher stands on his rear leg and twists his body to one side.

2. Cocking
He takes a long stride forwards on his front leg.

3. Acceleration
The body rotates as the arm comes over the shoulder. This movement combines with the straightening of the arm to produce the maximum speed at the point of release.

4. Follow through
The arm decelerates as the body catches up. The pitcher can no longer affect the ball, but this phase is important to ensure he does not injure himself.

TRY THIS

Using a tennis ball, see how using your body can help you throw a ball. First, stand facing the front with your feet together and keep the rest of your body still while you throw using just your arm. Now step back with the foot on the side of your throwing arm and turn your body to the side. As you throw, step forwards with the rear foot, turning your hips.

How much further can you throw when you add the step? Throw the ball at different angles and see how far it goes. Which angle produces the maximum distance?

Fun of the fair

Fairground rides give us a feeling of danger by doing seemingly impossible things, like turning us sideways or upside down. The rides are much safer than they feel due to the forces they produce.

Centripetal force

When we move in circles, a constant force acts on us towards the centre of the circle. This is called centripetal force, and it is the biggest key in understanding many roller coasters and fairground rides.

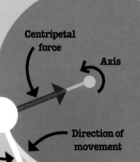

Centripetal force

Axis

Direction of velocity

Direction of movement

Rollercoaster ride

Rollercoaster cars are pulled to the top of the ride, giving them **potential energy**. From then on, the whole ride is powered by the force of gravity.

1. Maximum potential energy at start of ride.

2. Maximum kinetic energy just as car passes through bottom of loop.

Wall of Death

On the Wall of Death, daredevil motorcyclists ride round and round a **circular vertical wall**. They stay up the wall because **the force of friction** at the tyres **is equal to the force of gravity** pulling them down. However, the force of gravity acts from a point called the centre of gravity, away from the wall. This produces a force called **torque**, which tries to rotate the bike. To counter the torque, the rider leans up the wall. The reaction from the wall produces torque in the opposite direction to balance the bike.

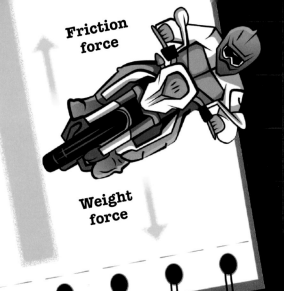

Friction force

Weight force

Upside-down

The loop on a rollercoaster is in a shape called a **clothoid loop**, which has a much tighter curve at the top than at the bottom. The riders are only fully upside-down for an instant. At that point, the track is hardly pressing on the car, and the riders feel like they are weightless. The tight curve ensures that riders are not upside-down for long, so nobody falls out.

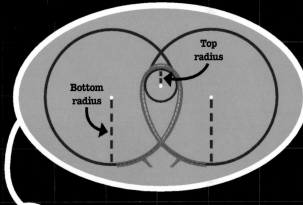

Top radius

Bottom radius

3. The top of each rise is lower than the start of the ride.

4. Centripetal force provided by track pushing against car allows it to "loop the loop".

5. The car has less energy at the end of the ride than at the start due to friction and air resistance.

Quiz

1 An astronaut in his spacesuit has a

mass of 250 kg.

On the Moon, he weighs **400 Newtons** in his suit. If the spacesuit has a **mass of 150 kg**, how many Newtons would the astronaut weigh on the Moon without his spacesuit? *Hint: First work out the mass of the astronaut, then compare this to his mass in his spacesuit.*

2 What is the name of the

energy

that an object has because **it is moving**?

3 What is the name for the **friction** caused when an object moves

through the air?

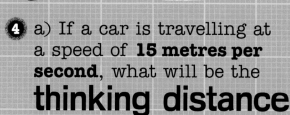

4 a) If a car is travelling at a speed of **15 metres per second**, what will be the

thinking distance

for stopping the car if it takes the driver $2/3$ second to apply the brakes?

"So, when do I need to brake?"

b) If the car's **braking distance** travelling at 15 metres per second is **12 metres**, what will its braking distance be at 30 metres per second?

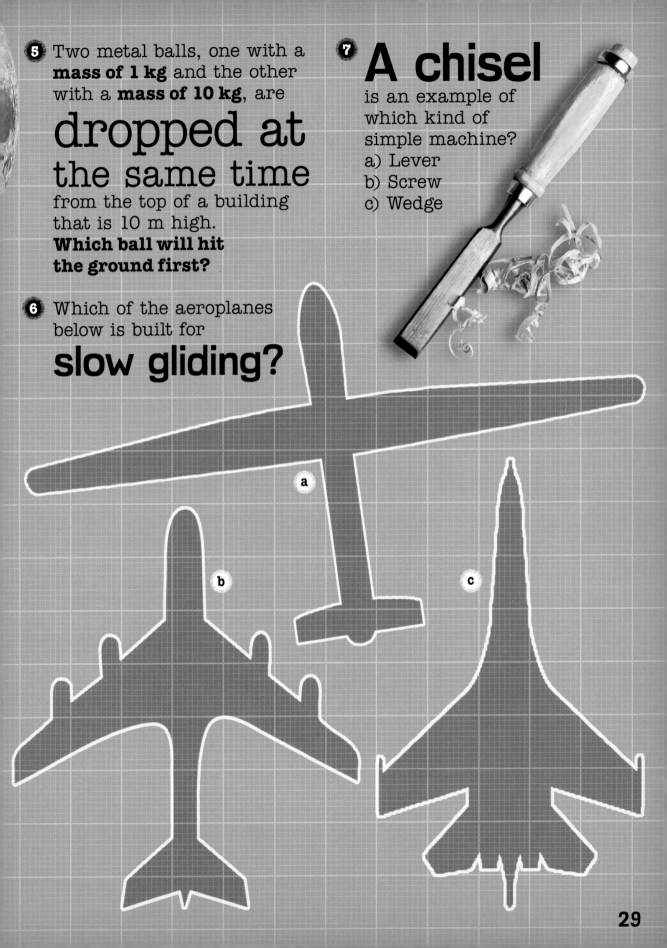

5 Two metal balls, one with a **mass of 1 kg** and the other with a **mass of 10 kg**, are

dropped at the same time

from the top of a building that is 10 m high. **Which ball will hit the ground first?**

6 Which of the aeroplanes below is built for

slow gliding?

7 # A chisel

is an example of which kind of simple machine?
a) Lever
b) Screw
c) Wedge

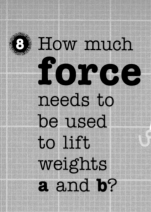

8 How much **force** needs to be used to lift weights **a** and **b**?

a b

200 Newtons 80 Newtons

9 Which of the following **bicycle gear ratios** would be best to cycle up a steep hill? (The ratios are written with the driver gear first, driven gear second.)
a) 2:1 b) 1:1 c) 1:2

11 What **class of lever** is each of the following?

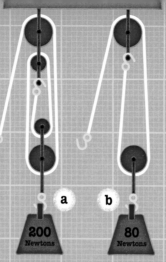

a) Tweezers
b) Seesaw

c) Nutcracker

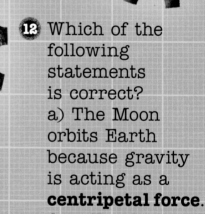

1

4

12 Which of the following statements is correct?
a) The Moon orbits Earth because gravity is acting as a **centripetal force**.
b) The Moon orbits Earth because there is **no gravity in space**.
c) The Moon orbits Earth because it is **attracted by the gravity** of other planets.

10 If **gear 1** turns in a **clockwise** direction, in which direction does **gear 4** turn?

Glossary

Acceleration
A change in an object's velocity, caused by applying a force.

Aerofoil
The curved shape of a wing, which generates lift.

Centripetal force
A force that acts on an object moving in circles.

Derailleur gears
A gear system consisting of a chain and gears of different sizes.

Friction
A force between two surfaces that slide against each other. Friction acts in the opposite direction to an object's movement, slowing it down.

Fulcrum
The point on which a lever turns.

Gear
A toothed wheel that interlocks with another toothed part of a machine to transfer motion.

Gradient
The angle of an inclined plane.

Gravity
The force of attraction between objects with mass.

Inclined plane
Also called a ramp, a sloping surface that is used to raise or lower objects.

Kinetic energy
The energy an object has due to its speed of movement.

Lever
A simple machine consisting of an arm that pivots at a fulcrum. Levers change the amount of force needed to move objects.

Lift
A force that acts on an object to push it in an upwards direction.

Mass
The amount of matter contained in an object.

Potential energy
A form of energy that an object has due to its height above the ground.

Pulley
A simple machine consisting of a wheel and a rope, which changes the direction of a force. Systems of two or more pulleys reduce the force needed to lift a load.

Torque
A force that causes an object to rotate.

Velocity
An object's speed in a particular direction.

Weight
The amount of force that gravity exerts on an object. An object's weight is proportional to its mass.

Index

Answers

1. 160 Newtons. Without his spacesuit, the astronaut has a mass of 100 kg. This is $100/250$ his weight with his spacesuit on. His weight is therefore $100/250 \times 400$ Newtons = 160 Newtons.
2. Kinetic energy
3. Air resistance
4. a) 10 metres b) 48 metres
5. This is a trick question. They will both hit the ground at the same time.
6. a)
7. c)
8. a) 50 N b) 40 N
9. a)
10. Anti-clockwise
11. a) Class 3 b) Class 1 c) Class 2
12. a)